Tom's Telescope

A Book about the Moon and the Sun

BY KERRY DINMONT

Published by The Child's World®
1980 Lookout Drive • Mankato, MN 56003-1705
800-599-READ • www.childsworld.com

Photographs ©: Shutterstock Images, cover, 1, 4–5, 7, 11, 13, 14;
Sandratsky Dmitriy/Shutterstock Images, 3; Mihai-Bogdan Lazar/
Shutterstock Images, 8; iStockphoto, 16–17, 21; Marcel Clemens/
Shutterstock Images, 18

Design Elements: Claudio Divizia/Shutterstock Images

ISBN 9781503820173
LCCN 2016960940

Printed in the United States of America
PA02339

Today, Tom got a telescope!

4

What will he see?

Tom wants to see the sun. The sun is very bright.

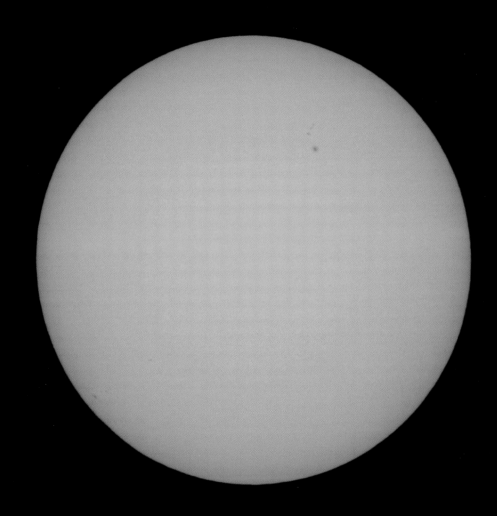

8

Tom needs a **filter** on his telescope. It keeps his eyes safe.

Earth **orbits** the sun.

11

Tom looks through his telescope at night. He sees lots of stars.

13

14

Tom sees the moon, too. The moon shines bright at night.

The moon is close to Earth.

Tom can see its **craters**.

18

The moon orbits Earth.

What would you look

at with a telescope?

Words to Know

craters (KRAY-turz) Craters are large holes. The moon has craters from space objects hitting it.

filter (FIL-ter) A filter blocks something out. We can only view the sun through a telescope if there is a filter to block the sun's light.

orbits (OR-bits) When something orbits, it moves in a circle around something else. Earth orbits the sun.

Extended Learning Activities

1 Have you ever looked through a telescope? What did you see?

2 Which words in this book have you never heard before? What clues in the text helped you understand their meaning?

3 Think of a time you looked at the moon. What did you see? What was its shape?

To Learn More

Books

Bauer, Marion Dane. *Sun*. New York, NY: Simon Spotlight, 2016.

Hughes, Catherine D. *First Big Book of Space*. Washington, DC: National Geographic, 2012.

Morgan, Emily R. *Next Time You See the Moon*. Arlington, VA: NSTA Kids, National Science Teachers Association, 2014.

Web Sites

Visit our Web site for links about the moon and the sun: **childsworld.com/links**

Note to Parents, Teachers, and Librarians: We routinely verify our Web links to make sure they are safe and active sites. So encourage your readers to check them out!

About the Author

Kerry Dinmont is a children's book author who enjoys art and nature. She lives in Montana with her two Norwegian elkhounds.